SUPERHEROES OF
NATURE

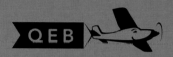

CONTENTS

INTRODUCTION

From Batman to Spiderman, the superheroes we have invented for ourselves—indestructible, always victorious—are so often inspired by animals.

Our fictional superheroes often lead a double life: unremarkable in the day-to-day world but miraculous in a crisis. In the animal world, many creatures mirror this behavior: sometimes they are modest and quiet; other times they act like stars. Often animals amaze us with their genius acrobatic moves, their ability to dodge enemies deftly, or their skill at disappearing using camouflage.

Compared to humans, nature's superheroes have mind-boggling powers of survival and defence. If we look closely at these powers, we can see how they are products of evolution, developed as adaptations to environmental pressures. Together, nature's superheroes show us the incredible biodiversity—variety of living things—that can be found on our planet. As well as celebrating nature's superheroes, this book also draws attention to the speed with which they are disappearing. As humans continue to destroy plant and animal habitats, hunt animals, and spread pollution, this book asks us to remember the kinds of life we risk losing.

Denis ODY, Oceanologist, WWF France

FEARSOME CREATURES

Through evolution, some animals have developed into fearsome fighters.

Whether predator or prey, an animal must hunt for food and not get eaten. Poisons, bloodsuckers, and skewers are just some of the incredible tools animals have developed over time to help them capture other creatures and defend themselves. The goal is always survival of the species. Of all the survival tricks and techniques that animals possess, the two most impressive are camouflage and poison, and both can be used in some surprising ways…

HORNED LIZARD

SUPERHERO QUALITY:
EYES OF BLOOD

SUPER STATS:
SCIENTIFIC NAME: *Phrynosoma cornutum*
FAMILY: *Phrynosomatidae*
Size: 3.5–6 inches (9–15 centimeters)
Weight: 0.7–3 ounces (20–90 grams)
Habitat: dry and semi-arid places
Location: North America

SUPER FACT:
This thorny reptile can blow itself up like a balloon!

When this creature wants to scare its enemies, it shoots jets of blood from its eyes!

The horned lizard, also known as Tapaya, lives in the deserts of North America. You can recognise it by the two elaborately patterned horns that encase its bulging eyes. It's large size and devilish looks—rather like a thorn-covered toad—are sometimes enough to put off predators. But coyotes will attack. To defend itself, the horned lizard spurts a jet of blood from its eyes with great accuracy. It can shoot this mixture of blood and a foul-tasting chemical from up to three feet away. It can also inflate its body to twice its normal size.

To capture prey—insects, centipedes and spiders—the horned lizard stays as still as a rock; then it pounces and gobbles up the creature in seconds.

BLUE POISON DART FROG

- **SUPERHERO QUALITY:**
  POISONOUS TO PREDATORS

- **SUPER STATS:**
  SCIENTIFIC NAME: *Dendrobates azureus*
  FAMILY: *Dendrobatidae*
  Size: 1.2–1.8 inches (3–4.5 centimeters)
  Weight: approx. 0.3 ounce (8 grams)
  Location: South America

- **SUPER FACT:**
  For such a tiny creature, this frog contains a large amount of poison.

The blue poison dart frog's striking color attracts all kinds of predators, from birds to small mammals and reptiles.

But any creature who swallows this little frog will regret it for a long time, if it doesn't die first! A lucky predator will find the taste of the frog so disgusting that it will spit the creature out, and that may save its life. If it survives, it will have learnt a valuable lesson; it won't try to catch this species again. A predator who swallows it may die, as the frog's skin contains a scary amount of poisonous chemicals, particularly alkaloids.

There are many brightly colored frogs in the rainforest, but not all are poisonous. Sometimes a harmless creature will mimic a brightly colored poisonous animal in order to ward off predators, a defence mechanism called "Batesian mimicry."

TAMANDUA

SUPERHERO QUALITY:
FEARLESS BOXER

SUPER STATS:
SCIENTIFIC NAME: *Tamandua tetradactyla*
FAMILY: *Myrmecophagidae*
Size: 4 feet (1.2 meters)
Diet: termites, ants, and bees

SUPER FACT:
The tamandua is not afraid of anything!

The size of a large cat, when threatened this South American anteater stands like a boxer on its hind legs to defend itself. No leather gloves for this guy, though; instead, it has impressive claws that could badly injure an aggressor.

A predator will generally attack the tamandua when it's on the ground hunting for termites, ants, or even bees to eat. This last snack gives it the nickname "honey bear." It has some impressive tools for catching its prey: powerful claws for breaking open the mounds where they live, and a 16-inch (40-cm) long, sticky tongue that it sticks into the tunnels in the mounds to collect the insects.

When not hunting, the tamandua seeks safety in the trees, where it uses its feet and tail to hang from branches. Most of its digestion takes place at night, when the glands in its butt secrete a sticky liquid. Even if you can't see it in the dark, you—and predators such as jaguars—will definitely be able to smell it and will want to run a mile!

LICHEN KATYDID

 SUPERHERO QUALITY:
MASTER IMITATOR

 **SUPER STATS:**
SCIENTIFIC NAME: *Markia hystrix*
FAMILY: *Tettigoniidae*
Size: 0.4–2.3 inches
(1–6 centimeters)
Location: South America

 SUPER FACT:
On lichen, this katydid's features conceal it as effectively as an invisibility cloak.

Katydid grasshoppers use camouflage to make themselves vanish before their predators' very eyes!

This particular species has a body that bristles with white spikes and threads resembling the tree-bark lichen on which it lives and feeds. It relies on camouflage to protect it from any birds, lizards, or frogs that might want to make it their dinner. Any predator would have to look very hard to spot its insect features, such as antennae, wings, or legs. The only thing that might give it away is its very slow movements. It took a long process of evolution for this grasshopper to refine its disguise so successfully.

Other katydid grasshoppers have evolved a different form of camouflage; they look just like leaves! Some even look like decayed or speckled leaves; no two look the same! This makes it harder for predators to spot them hiding on plants.

TETRADON

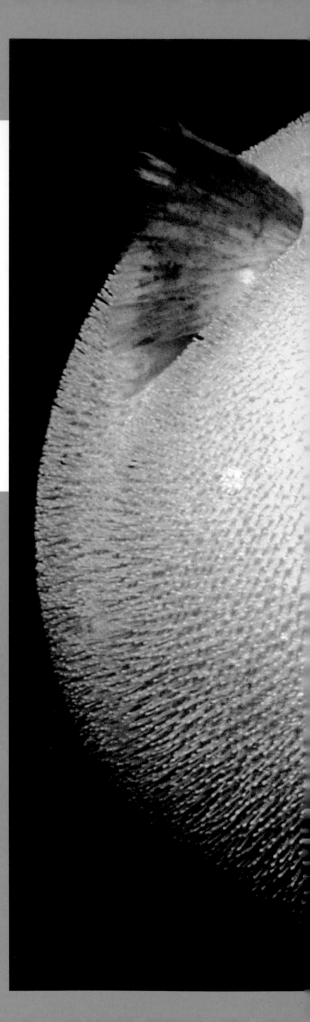

💪 **SUPERHERO QUALITY:**
INFLATABLE BODY

💡 **SUPER STATS:**
SCIENTIFIC NAME: *Arothron meleagris*
FAMILY: *Tetraodontidae*
Size: 12–20 inches (30–50 centimeters)
Diet: coral, sea-sponges, and mollusks
Location: Indian Ocean

👍 **SUPER FACT:**
"Tetra" in this fish's name is a Greek word meaning "four;" it refers to the fish's four teeth, which can give a painful bite!

As soon as it senses aggression, this fish blows itself up to make itself bigger—so much so that it's earned the nickname "globe fish!"

It does this by swallowing a huge amount of water, which fills its expandable stomach. A membrane at the back of its mouth stops the water from flowing out again. While inflated, predators will stay away from this gigantic ball. The downside is, the tetradon can't swim off!

The globe fish has another defence mechanism though: certain parts of its body—mainly its eyes, liver, and ovaries—are extremely poisonous. The poison, called "tetrodotoxin," paralyzes the muscles of anything that swallows it. In Japan, globe fish or "fugu" are cooked as a speciality dish. You need to be a real expert to tell which parts can be eaten and which parts are poisonous. Every year, several people die after taking the risk of eating fugu!

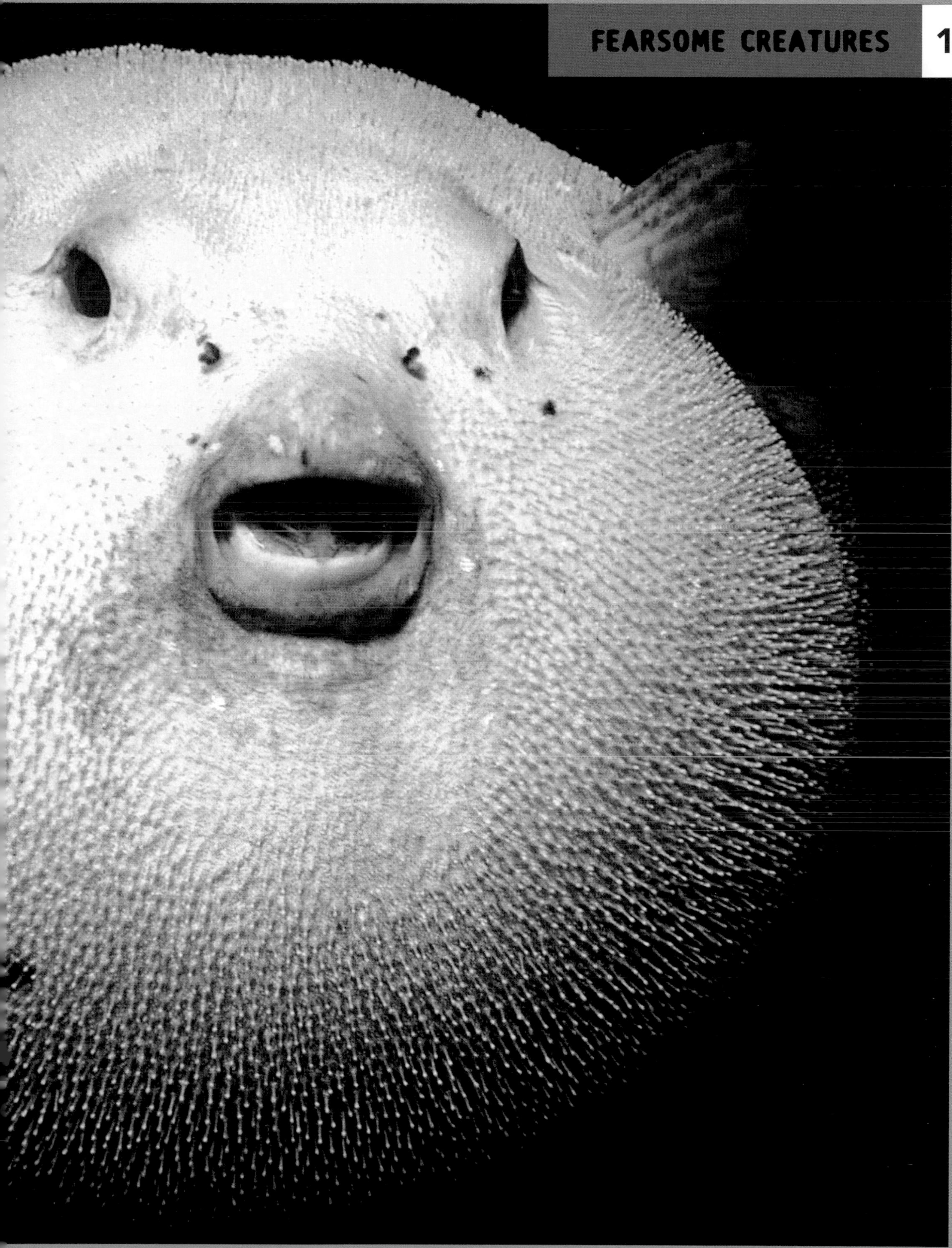

HONEY BADGER

 **SUPERHERO QUALITY:**
TOTALLY FEARLESS

SUPER STATS:
SCIENTIFIC NAME:
Mellivora capensis
Size: 20–27.5 inches
(50–70 centimeters)
Location: India, the Arabian
peninsula, and sub-Saharan
Africa (except Madagascar)

 SUPER FACT:
The honey badger
can run backward, a
useful skill when facing
attackers very much
larger than itself!

Weighing no more than 33 pounds (15 kilograms), the honey badger can take on prey as large as buffaloes!

This has earned it the nickname "terror of the savannah." It usually only resorts to such large prey if there are food shortages. At other times, it loves to eat bee larvae and honey. A popular belief suggests it has cultivated a useful friendship with a bird called the honeyguide. This bird is said to point it to where there is a wild hive down on the ground. The honey badger finds the hive and demolishes it; stings don't bother it! After it has eaten its fill, the little bird flies down and eats up the leftovers.

The honey badger can also eat poisons that would be fatal to humans. While still young, it slowly builds up its resistance to poisons by eating scorpions and little snakes such as vipers. By the time it is full grown, it can catch and eat much larger snakes, such as the deadly black mamba.

BORNEO ANT

SUPERHERO QUALITY:
NOBLE SELF-DESTRUCTION

SUPER STATS:
SCIENTIFIC NAME: *Colobopsis explodens*
FAMILY: *Formicidae*
Color: brownish-red
Location: Borneo, Malaysia

SUPER FACT:
The Borneo ant has no sting.

To save its colony, this extraordinary ant can make itself explode!

This species was recently discovered in the treetops of Borneo. Like most ants, it lives in a colony with a queen and millions of workers. Soldier ants defend the colony. Some of the soldier ants are sturdy, with a shieldlike head and powerful pincers. These strong soldier ants defend the colony by fighting. Others are more delicately built and have a more surprising weapon. As soon as they see a threat, they will scrunch up their abdomen. This bursts a pouch in their belly, spraying a toxic, slimy, yellow substance at the enemy. Having exploded, the ant dies!

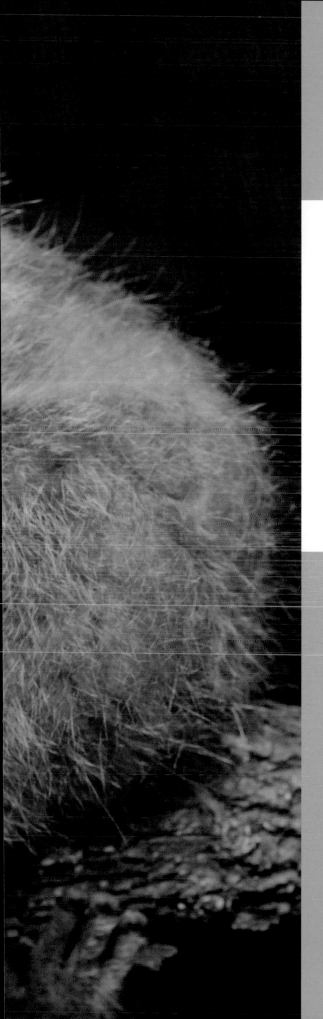

PYGMY SLOW LORIS

SUPERHERO QUALITY:
DECEPTIVE CUTENESS

SUPER STATS:
SCIENTIFIC NAME: *Nycticebus pygmaeus*
FAMILY: *Lorisidae*
Size: 7–9 inches (19–23 centimeters)
Weight: 16 ounces (450 grams)
Location: Southeast Asia

SUPER FACT:
Pygmy and other slow lorises are the only primates that use venom for defence.

If any predator comes near, the pygmy slow loris covers its teeth in a powerful poison!

The poison is made by glands near its elbows. Lifting up its arms, it licks the parts where the venom is made, then uses its tongue to spread the toxic substance around its mouth. Its poison-coated teeth can give a painful bite. Although a pygmy slow loris bite wouldn't kill a human, it would certainly trigger a reaction like a bad allergy.

The deceptively cute appearance of this loris has caused it big problems. Captured from the forests in large numbers, it is sold to pet traders. Even worse, humans are destroying its habitat by cutting down trees, and it is now endangered. Other slow loris species in India and Cambodia are threatened for the same reasons.

LOWLAND STREAKED TENREC

SUPERHERO QUALITY:
VIBRATING QUILLS

SUPER STATS:
SCIENTIFIC NAME: *Hemicentetes semispinosus*
Size: 6–7.5 inches (16–19 centimeters)
Location: Madagascar

SUPER FACT:
Lowland streaked tenrecs make sounds that humans cannot hear.

This little creature defends itself with spikes or "quills" that make a noise.

If attacked, it sticks its detachable quills into the skin of its attacker and leaves them there. Female tenrecs will even do this to males if they don't want them to come too close! Its stripes provide excellent camouflage in the long grass.

By vibrating specialized quills on its back, the tenrec can make high-pitched ultrasound calls similar to the noises made by bats. If a young tenrec gets lost, it can "call" to its parents this way. Tenrecs also use ultrasounds to ward off predators, especially mongooses.

EYED ELECTRIC RAY

💪 **SUPERHERO QUALITY:**
SUPER-ENERGETIC

💡 **SUPER STATS:**
SCIENTIFIC NAME: *Torpedo torpedo*
FAMILY: *Torpedinidae*
Size: 23.6 inches (60 centimeters)
Location: Mediterranean Sea and the eastern Atlantic Ocean

👍 **SUPER FACT:**
The ancient Greeks and Romans made medicines from this electric fish.

This disk-shaped ray can give electric shocks of up to 200 volts!

It does this to defend itself and to stun prey. Well camouflaged, it spends much of its time buried on the seabed, where its brown and orange back blends in so well with the sand that it becomes almost invisible. Only the dark blue circles, or "eyes," on its back stand out. When a prey fish passes, it pounces and stuns it with electricity, then swallows it whole. The eyed electric ray generates electricity by contracting its muscles. It stores the electric charge in two large organs located under its skin on either side of its head. The organs, which are made up of specialized cells called electrocytes, act like a battery. If a predator touches the ray or gets too close, trying to tell if this flat object is actually food, the ray delivers a series of rapid electric pulses that gives the predator a nasty shock—strong enough to knock a person off their feet!

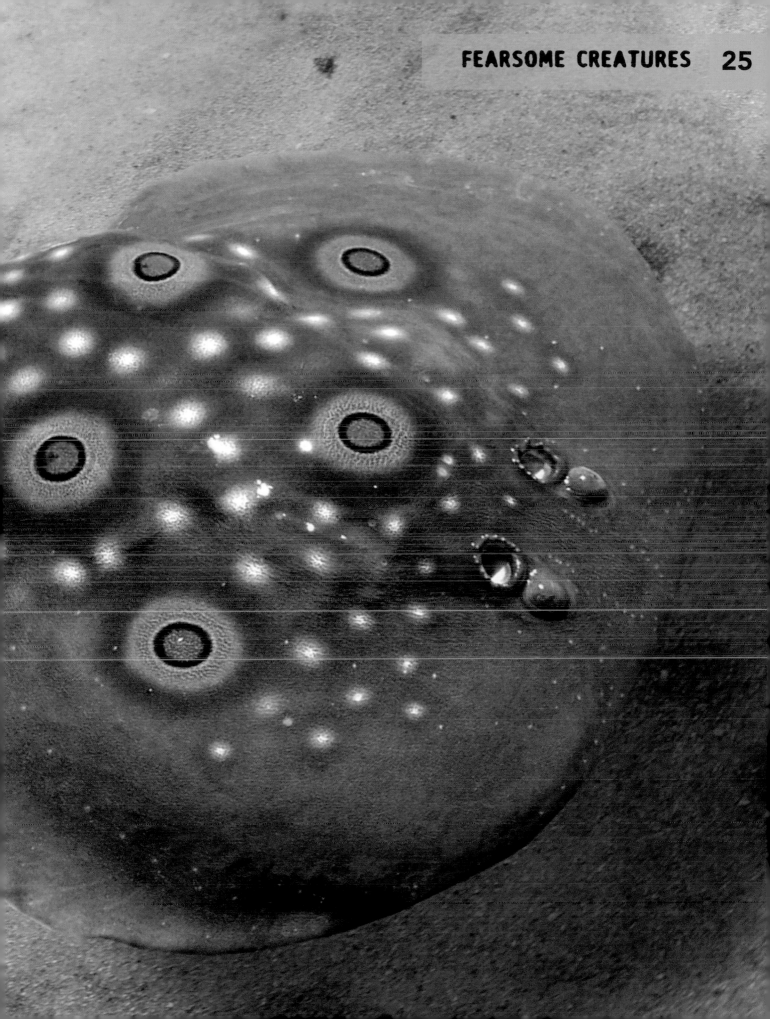

SUPER WORKERS

Some animals will selflessly take on the jobs that are most beneficial to their communities.

These worker animals go to incredible lengths to build protective environments, hunt for food, or ensure that their communities are safe. Some will take on the role of guides or lookouts, putting themselves in danger to defend their family or community. Others are outstanding builders and architects, working tirelessly to build complex burrow systems, giant nests, or huge earth mounds. These miniature "cities" may be home to millions of individuals.

LEAF-CUTTER ANTS

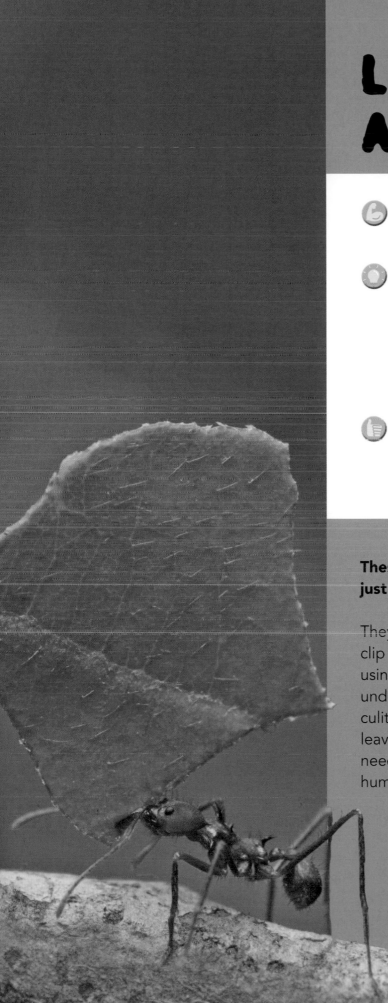

SUPERHERO QUALITY:
WORLD-CLASS FARMERS

SUPER STATS:
TRIBE: Attini
Number of species: 39
Habitat: humid tropical and subtropical areas (forests, savannas)
Location: Central and South America

SUPER FACT:
Leaf-cutter ants can carry pieces of leaf many times their own size.

These ants can strip all the leaves from a tree in just one day!

They don't eat them, though! Instead, they clip them into large pieces, which they carry—using their incredibly strong jaws—back to their underground nest. Deep within the nest, the ants cultivate a fungus that grows on the chewed leaves and feeds off their nutrients. The fungus needs very specific temperatures and levels of humidity, and provides the ants with their own food source.

Leaf-cutter colonies can grow to several million individuals—that's lots of mouths to feed! So when a big tree falls, the ants move quickly to strip it. This lets light into the forest, helping younger trees to grow.

ARCTIC TERN

🖐 **SUPERHERO QUALITY:**
POLAR PILOT

⬡ **SUPER STATS:**
SCIENTIFIC NAME: *Sterna paradisaea*
FAMILY: *Laridae*
Size: 12–20 inches (30–50 centimeters)
Wingspan: 29.5–33.5 inches (75–85 centimeters)
Life expectancy: 20–30 years

👍 **SUPER FACT:**
The long-lived arctic tern lives in an eternal summer.

This migratory bird flies from the North Pole to the South Pole and back every year. No other bird can do that!

The arctic tern breeds in the Arctic in summer. In winter, it flies to Antarctica, where it's about to be summer. So for this lucky bird, it is always summer! It gets its energy from a diet of fish and crustaceans, and flies a zigzag route using the trade winds, which blow toward the equator. This way it can travel 22,000 miles (35,000 kilometers) each year.

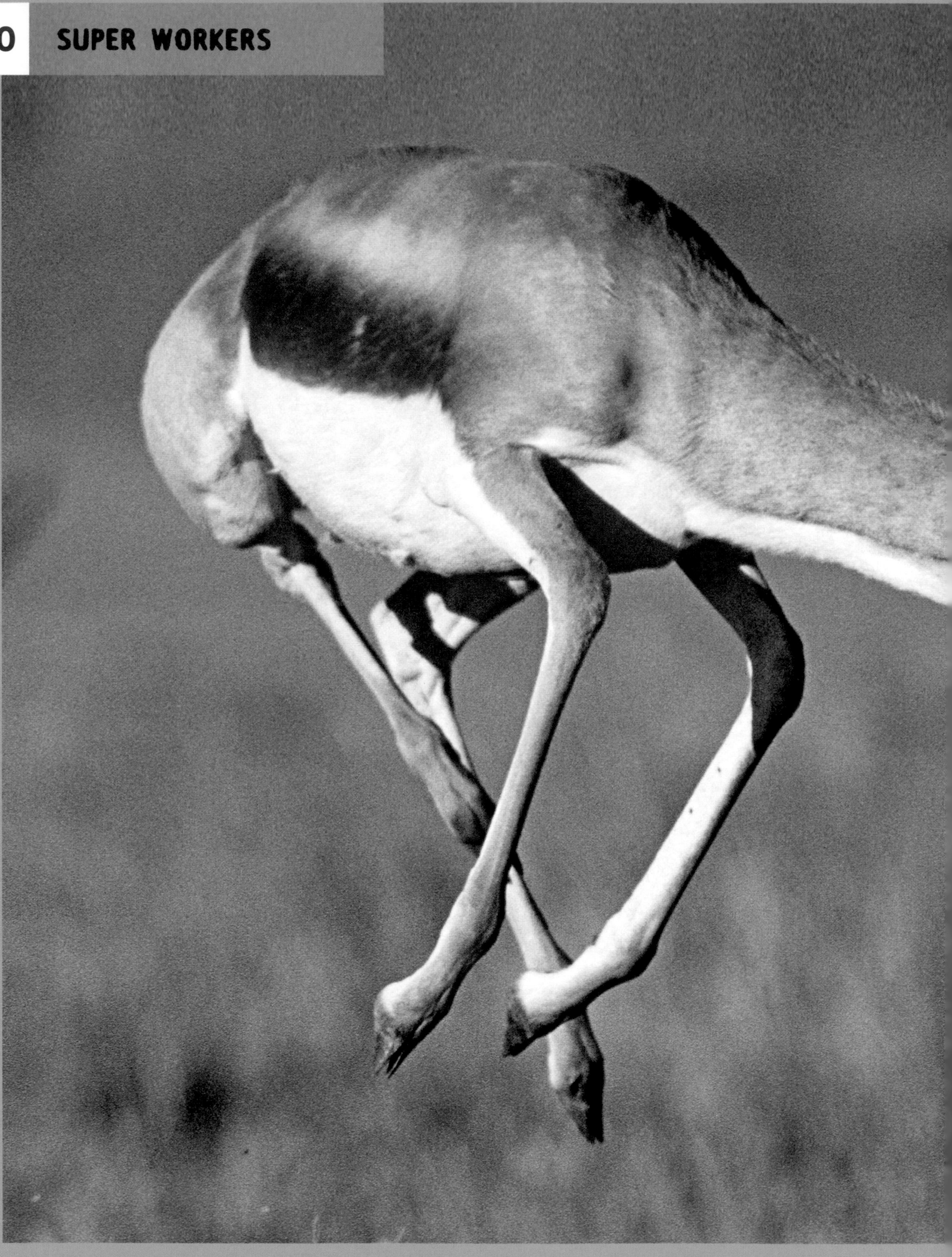

SPRINGBOK

💪 **SUPERHERO QUALITY:**
SUPER SPRINGY

💡 **SUPER STATS:**
SCIENTIFIC NAME: *Antidorcas marsupialis*
FAMILY: *Bovidae*
Height: 29–35 inches (75–90 centimeters)
Location: Southern Africa

👍 **SUPER FACT:**
The South African rugby team adopted the springbok as its symbol because of its incredible speed and agility.

Using its back legs like springs, the springbok can jump 13 feet (4 meters) high and leap an impressive 49 feet (15 meters) forward!

In its savanna home, which it shares with some of Africa's most fearsome predators, it lives on constant high alert, using its super-accute senses to detect the presence of lions, leopards, and cheetahs. These predators are particularly keen on the gazelle's tender, muscly flesh.

If an enemy looks ready to attack, the springbok will make a run for it. Moving super-fast—about 31 miles per hour (50 kilometers per hour) over long distances—it runs and bounds in zig-zags to confuse the chaser. On a short sprint it can reach 62 miles per hour (100 kilometers per hour)! The reason it bounces so well is because its back legs are folded in a "Z" shape, its tendons and ligaments are exceptionally flexible, and its muscles are extremely well toned.

BLACK WILDEBEEST

 **SUPERHERO QUALITY:**
BRAVE LEADER

 SUPER STATS:
SCIENTIFIC NAME:
Connochaetes gnou
Length: 59–79 inches
(150–200 centimeters)
Weight 240–595 pounds
(110–270 kilograms)
Life expectancy: 15–20 years

SUPER FACT:
Wildebeests and zebras team up to migrate together, grazing and traveling as a pack.

Not all wildebeests are heroes, but the leaders of the pack certainly are.

In August, wildebeests—several hundred thousand of them—and zebras leave the plains of the Serengeti in Tanzania for the green grasslands of the Masai Mara in Kenya. A keen sense of smell helps them find their way as they migrate toward the savannas. Packs of lions, leopards, and cheetahs follow them on their journey, but kill only a tiny proportion of the pack.

A much greater danger for them is the river Mara, which they must swim across. Scared to jump in, they circle around and around on the riverbank, until one brave leader summons up the courage to jump. As soon as one wildebeest takes the plunge and starts to swim across, the rest follow, driven by the instinct to survive. Many will get swept away by the strong current and drown; others will get eaten by crocodiles. But the majority of wildebeests will make it safely to the other side.

SOCIABLE WEAVER

SUPERHERO QUALITY:
SUPER-ARCHITECT

SUPER STATS:
SCIENTIFIC NAME: *Philetairus socius*
FAMILY: *Ploceidae*
Size: 5.5 inches (14 centimeters)
Weight: 0.9–1.1 ounces (26–30 grams)
Habitat: arid zones
Location: South Africa

SUPER FACT:
Sociable weavers live in nests with multiple bedrooms.

This hero of collective living builds nests of record-breaking size for up to 500 birds!

The birds themselves are small, about the size of a sparrow, and have a cone-shaped beak adapted for eating grains.

When it's time to build a nest, sociable weavers work together to construct them on poles and overhead lines, and in trees. Each nest is divided into rooms. The rooms in the middle are warmer, for sleeping; those on the outside let the breeze in, so the birds use them on hot days to keep cool. These nests can be up to 16 feet (5 meters) long and weigh several tons. Branches have been known to break under the weight of sociable weaver nests!

EEL

💪 **SUPERHERO QUALITY:**
GENIUS NAVIGATOR

💡 **SUPER STATS:**
SCIENTIFIC NAME: *Anguilla anguilla*
FAMILY: *Anguillidae*
Size: 16–59 inches (40–150 centimeters)
Weight: up to 9 pounds (4 kilograms)

👍 **SUPER FACT:**
The eel travels about 5,000 miles (8,000 kilometers) between birth and mating.

Eels can navigate thousands of miles thanks to their incredible sense of smell!

They are born in the Sargasso Sea, a patch of ocean in the western Atlantic (the only sea without a land boundary). From there, the young eels drift all the way to the coast of Europe. If they manage to escape the fishermen who are waiting there with nets, they swim up the rivers, such as those flowing from the Pyrenees, filling up on little fish as they go. By the time they reach adulthood, they can be up to 59 inches long! Eventually, the eels let themselves be carried by the current down to the estuaries, where they swim back out into the Atlantic. Guided by smell—even a single molecule can be enough to point an eel in the right direction—they make their incredible journey back to their birthplace, where they mate.

Although eels lay an enormous number of eggs, many don't survive. Add to this overfishing, and they are now an endangered species.

BEAVERS

SUPERHERO QUALITY:
SKILLED CARPENTERS

SUPER STATS:
FAMILY: *Castoridae*
Size: Eurasian beaver 29–53 inches (73–135 centimeters); North American beaver 35–46 inches (90–117 centimeters)
Habitat: wooded river banks

SUPER FACT:
The beaver remodels the woodland environment to suit itself!

These semi-aquatic rodents are skilled carpenters, builders, and architects!

Both North American and Eurasian beavers have powerful incisor teeth that keep growing throughout their lives. They use their teeth to cut down trees, even ones with huge trunks. Having felled a tree, to keep its teeth sharp the beaver gnaws on the trunk while turning it, as if sharpening a giant pencil. It also eats the succulent leaves that once grew at the top of the tree.

Beavers use the felled trees to build dams. This allows them to control the flow of the river. First, they carry logs into the water and fix them firmly in the riverbed. Then they pile branches and mud on top of the logs to keep the structure together. The Eurasian beaver—the smaller of the two species—makes dams up to 100 feet (30 meters) long, while its North American cousin makes them even longer! As well as being a good builder, the Eurasian beaver is also a skilled architect, digging complex burrows in the riverbank.

MASTERS OF SEDUCTION

To keep a species going, females must give birth to the next generation, but first they must be enticed by the males to mate.

Nature has given animals an array of wildly different powers of seduction to help them attract a mate. Some of their more surprising characteristiscs or habits are designed to make the creature stand out from the crowd: bright colors, elaborate mating dances, serenades—even big noses! Often, but not always, it's the males of the species that use the more outlandish methods of attraction.

ELEPHANT SEALS

💪 **SUPERHERO QUALITY:**
MACHO MONARCHS

🏅 **SUPER STATS:**
FAMILY: *Phocidae*
Height: approx. 16 feet (5 meters), male;
8 feet (2.4 meters), female
Location: eastern Pacific, South Atlantic,
south Indian Ocean, Antarctica

👍 **SUPER FACT:**
Male elephant seals are about twice as tall
as females, and much heavier.

**The male elephant seal, the king of seals, has
a special trunk-shaped nose, used during the
mating season to produce very loud roars.**

The roars are made to put off other males that
might want to woo the same females. The females
are "guarded" by the leader of the pack. If a
young male tries to make a move on the females,
the leader will angrily chase him off.

Both northern and southern elephant seals are
diving champions. Some have been found as deep
as 3,280 feet (1,000 meters)! This ability allows
them to hunt for fish and squid in places other
predators cannot reach. Southern elephant seals
were once hunted to the brink of extinction for the
thick layer of fat under their skin. Today, there is a
good-sized population of southern elephant seals.
Northern elephant seals are protected.

CICADAS

💪 **SUPERHERO QUALITY:**
FAMOUS "SINGERS"

💡 **SUPER STATS:**
FAMILY: *Cicadidae*
Size: 2–3.5 inches (5–9 centimeters)
Color: green or brown
Species age: over 264 million years

👍 **SUPER FACT:**
African cicadas are record-breaking noise makers, making sounds of more than 150 decibels!

Male cicadas use tymbals to make a haunting, chirruping sound to impress females.

The tymbals are membranes located behind the male's wings on either side of its body. If you have ever pressed the domed bottom of a drink can to make a clicking noise (by popping the metal in and out), you'll have an idea how the cicada's tymbals work; it makes its clicking sounds by vibrating its membranes very fast. Because the male's abdomen is largely hollow, the sound resonates like a drum and is amplified. The female has a double-hearing organ in the second section of her abdomen to help her hear his noises. That's right—she hears with her belly!

The cicada's "song" has long been associated with the Mediterranean. However, because of climate change, these creatures can be heard making their sounds several miles further north each year.

PEACOCK SPIDER

SUPERHERO QUALITY:
CRAZY DANCER

SUPER STATS:
SCIENTIFIC NAME: *Maratus volans*
FAMILY: *Salticidae*
Size: approx. 0.2 inch (4 millimeters)
Location: Australia

SUPER FACT:
The peacock spider's abdomen is covered in scales that catch different wavelengths of light, making it shimmer.

To attract a female, the tiny male peacock spider—no bigger than a grain of rice—performs a frenzied dance.

He raises his abdomen, and also raises and fans out—rather like a peacock's tail—two brightly colored flaps on his abdomen. He also lifts and wiggles two of his legs. His dance not only signals to the female that he will be a good mate; it also stops her from eating him! If the female shows an interest, the male dances even more wildly, demonstrating his fine physique, which indicates they will have good offspring.

Peacock spiders are found in two parts of Australia: Queensland and New South Wales. Part of the jumping spider family, they stalk their prey, leap on it, and kill it with a fatal bite!

PROBOSCIS MONKEY

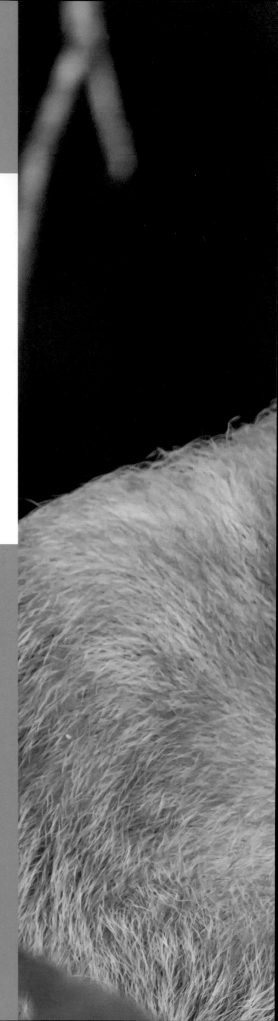

SUPERHERO QUALITY:
SUPER SEDUCER

SUPER STATS:
SCIENTIFIC NAME: *Nasalis larvatus*
FAMILY: *Cercopithecidae*
Size: 21–26 inches (53–67 centimeters)
Habitat: mangrove forests, close to
freshwater, and tropical lowland forests
Location: Borneo

SUPER FACT:
The proboscis monkey's nose turns red
when it is angry.

**For the male proboscis monkey, the longer his
nose, the more attractive he is to females!**

Only the males have this oversized feature, as if
to say: "Look at my big nose, a sure sign I'll have
beautiful offspring." The nose keeps growing all
the monkey's life, making the oldest monkeys the
most attractive. They also have a great sense of
smell! The monkeys communicate—for example,
sounding the alarm—with cries, which are
amplified in the space inside the nose. Females
have a much more modest nose.

Troops of proboscis monkeys live in the forests
of Borneo, where they spend all their time in the
trees. The group has a hierarchy determined by
behavior, but also by... size of nose! Habitat loss
from deforestation is their greatest threat.

GREATER SAGE GROUSE

🦾 **SUPERHERO QUALITY:**
BIG SHOW-OFF

💡 **SUPER STATS:**
SCIENTIFIC NAME: *Centrocercus urophasianus*
FAMILY: *Phasianidae*
Weight 3–6.5 pounds (1.5–3 kilograms)
Habitat: grasslands and sagebrush steppes of western North America

✊ **SUPER FACT:**
This species is the biggest grouse in North America.

This big bird puts on one of the most impressive courtship displays in the North American prairies!

The male uses several tricks to try and win the right to mate. First, he fans out his striking tail like a peacock, and makes strange gurgling noises. Then he puffs out his chest. His collar of white feathers may be beautiful, but more exciting to the female are the two yellow-green sacs on his throat that he inflates like an airbag. He moves these up and down while flapping his wings back and forth.

The brown-and-white speckled female is much less showy than the male. When she finally decides she is ready to mate, she crouches down. Sitting on her nest in the long grasses, her excellent camouflage helps to keep her safe from predators.

SURVIVORS

Creatures can thrive in all kinds of extreme conditions, both on land and in the ocean.

Although for us humans, environments such as deserts, ice, caves, and mountaintops are often too harsh for survival, to some animals and plants extreme heat and cold are no problem. Some creatures can survive with very little water; others are able to endure ferocious storms. There are even species that have survived global catastrophes, such as the meteorite strike that wiped out the dinosaurs, and major volcanic eruptions; these animals are a testament to the powers of survival in nature.

DUNG BEETLES

SUPERHERO QUALITY:
HYDRATION EXPERTS

SUPER STATS:
SUBFAMILY: *Scarabaeinae*
Diet: omnivore
Habitat: desert
Location: worldwide

SUPER FACT:
Desert-dwelling dung beetles capture dew drops with their backs!

Dung beetles are well known for their habit of eating poop!

All dung beetle species do this, and there are lots of them! The *Scarabaeinae* subfamily alone has more than 5,000 species in three main groups: rollers, dwellers, and tunnelers. The rollers collect dung by rolling it into large balls while walking backward. The dung is stored and used to feed their young.

Desert-dwelling dung beetles have another great survival trick. In the Namib desert, the beetles spend the day sheltering from the sun so they don't dehydrate. But at night, when it is cooler, they start to climb up the giant sand dunes; it takes them til morning to reach the top. Then, with their bodies tilted forward, they angle their backs toward the wind so they can catch any micro-droplets of spray blowing in from the ocean. Their morning drink is enough to keep them going all day!

KANGAROO RAT

 **SUPERHERO QUALITY:**

DISCIPLINED DIETER

 **SUPER STATS:**

SCIENTIFIC NAME:
Dipodomys deserti
Habitat: sandy deserts
Location: USA and Mexico

SUPER FACT:

With its oversized back legs, this bouncy rat looks like a mini kangaroo (although it is actually a rodent).

This little desert animal can survive for three years without water. Humans would struggle to survive three days!

The kangaroo rat gets whatever moisture it can from its food, and avoids dehydration by spending the day in its burrow out of the sun. At night, which can be chilly in the desert, it emerges to drink the dewdrops that form on plants.

To help it avoid dehydration, the kangaroo rat has developed several special adaptations. Its intestines, and most of all its kidneys, work to make sure that it doesn't excrete any water. Blood vessels around the intestine reabsorb all the moisture that gets to the stomach, so its droppings are completely dry. As for its pee, the kidneys filter out any water and send it back into the bloodstream.

FIRE SALAMANDER

SUPERHERO QUALITY:
SUPER-DEFENDER

SUPER STATS:
SCIENTIFIC NAME:
Salamandra salamandra
Lifespan: approx. 30 years
Habitat: humid areas
Location: central and southern Europe

SUPER FACT:
Salamanders are sometimes born live,
but sometimes hatch from eggs!

The fire salamander may not be the flameproof creature of ancient Roman legend, but it does have some remarkable powers of survival.

This modest amphibian can live for several decades, which is unusual for an animal so small. If it loses a limb, it can regrow it in just a few months. It also has some incredible antifreeze mechanisms that lower its freezing point and enable it to stay active all winter long. It achieves this by limiting blood flow to its legs and tail, and by producing a kind of sugar in its internal bodily fluids. The salamander's survival skills don't stop there. Its bright colors give a clear signal to potential predators: "Watch out! Eat me at your own risk!" In addition, behind its eyes it has two glands that produce a horrible-tasting poison. If a predator tries to eat it, it will quickly spit the salamander out. Too late though!

NAUTILUSES

SUPERHERO QUALITY:
LIVING FOSSILS

SUPER STATS:
FAMILY: *Nautilidae*
Size: 8–10 inches (20–26 centimeters)
Habitat: over 1,300 feet (400 meters) deep
Location: near Pacific islands and
Australian coasts

SUPER FACT:
Nautiluses have survived two great global catastrophes, including the one that killed off the dinosaurs.

These creatures (it's generally agreed there are four species) have lived through several geological eras without changing one bit!

Nautiluses and their cousins, squid and octopuses, are all cephalopod mollusks. Nautilus fossils from what's called the "primary era" have an identical structure to today's nautiluses. That means they haven't evolved in over 500 million years!

Why haven't nautiluses changed, when the vast majority of animal species have either evolved or died out? Maybe it's because they have always lived in perfect harmony with their tropical marine habitat. A nautilus can rise and sink thanks to an internal system of chambers, which are filled with gas. By adding or removing water, it can adjust how heavy or light it is. This enables it to move between deep zones, where it finds shelter, and the surface, where it goes to feed at night.

MUSK OX

 **SUPERHERO QUALITY:**

KING OF THE ICE

SUPER STATS:
SCIENTIFIC NAME: *Ovibos moschatus*
Height: 4.6–8 feet (1.4 meters)
Weight: 470–700 pounds (215–315 kilograms)
Location: Canada, Greenland

SUPER FACT:
This hairy animal may look like a buffalo, but it is more closely related to the goat family!

The musk ox has been around since the last ice age!

Adapted to extreme conditions, it lives in the Arctic Circle, where temperatures are often as low as -4 to -22 degrees Fahrenheit. It survives thanks to its super-thick fur. The hairs on its woolly fleece are up to 23 inches (60 centimeters) long. Musk ox live in herds, huddling close to each other to boost their protection from the cold. Super-sensitive to heat, it can't handle temperatures of 50 degrees Fahrenheit, so climate change poses a serious threat.

The male musk ox has horns that meet above its head and curve downward. This horn-helmet is handy in fights over females, or if a predator such as the Arctic wolf gets too close to the herd. To mark its territory, the male releases a strong-smelling substance called "musk," which comes out of a gland near its eyes.

MONARCH BUTTERFLY

💪 **SUPERHERO QUALITY:**
SUPER-MIGRATOR

💡 **SUPER STATS:**
SCIENTIFIC NAME: *Danaus plexippus*
FAMILY: *Nymphalidae*
Size: 3.3–4.9 inches (8.6–12.4 centimeters)
Location: the Americas

👍 **SUPER FACT:**
This strong-winged butterfly travels
3,000 miles (4,800 kilometers) a year
between the American continents.

**In a spectacular black-and-orange display,
monarch butterflies migrate thousands of
miles directed only by their genes!**

Every year, millions of them escape the harsh
winter in Canada and the United States for
warmer Mexico. Astonishingly, they go through
their reproductive cycle several times during
the journey; so it's the descendants of the
butterflies which came from the north that will
make the journey back there in the spring.

Monarch caterpillars feed on a poisonous
plant called milkweed, and absorb its
toxicity. The butterflies' bright colors
are a warning to predators that
they are poisonous. Sadly, pesticides
are reducing the numbers of these
magnificent butterflies.

TRUE ORIGINALS

Original, extraordinary, unusual-looking; some creatures just leave us speechless!

There's the star-nosed mole that can sniff out prey underwater; the jellyfish that can keep on regenerating itself; and the frog with a see-through body. Nature's inventiveness—the result of slow evolution—is simply breathtaking!

TREEHOPPERS

🦾 **SUPERHERO QUALITY:**
JUMPING MUTANTS

💡 **SUPER STATS:**
FAMILY: *Membracidae*
Number of species: 3,270
Location: worldwide; most diverse in
Central and South America

👍 **SUPER FACT:**
Some treehoppers lose their helmets
when fighting predators.

**The treehopper's strange-looking helmet is
actually a pair of modified wings!**

As with all insects, these sap-sucking creatures
have six legs and two pairs of wings. But, weirdly,
their helmets, which are not actually on their
heads, evolved from a third pair of wings! In most
insects, wing growth is controlled by a gene
called "hox," which stops wings from forming
anywhere other than the second and third
sections of the thorax. But in treehoppers, due
to a special quirk of evolution, the gene allows a
highly modified third pair of wings—the helmet
—to grow on the first section of the thorax.
The helmets are designed to deter predators
and provide camouflage. Some look like
thorns, ants, feather dusters, television
antenna, leaves, even helicopter wings!

Treehoppers communicate by shaking
their bodies and vibrating the surface
they are on. Other treehoppers pick up
the vibrations through their legs.

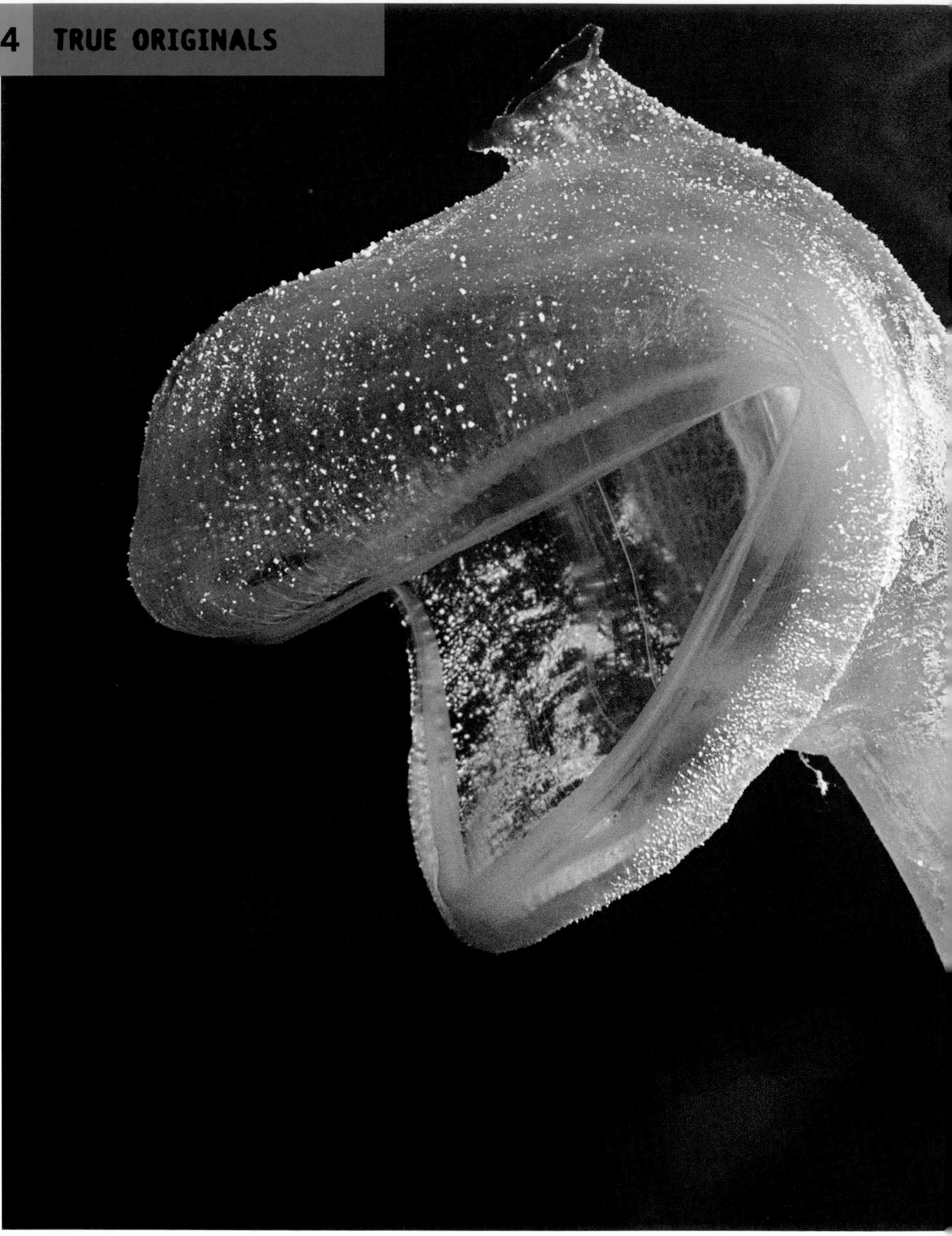

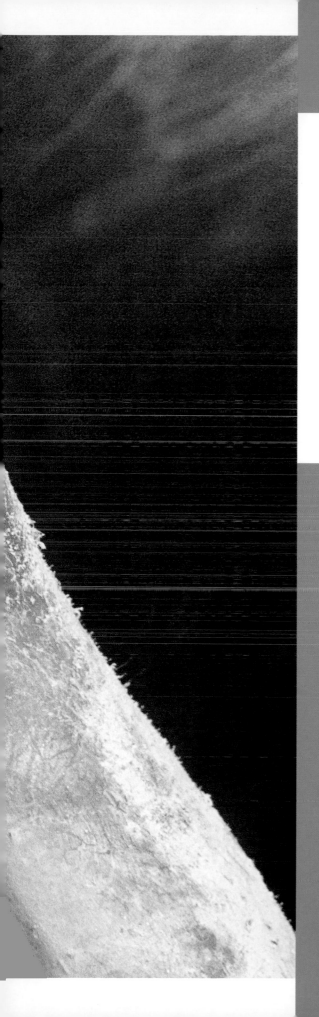

GHOSTFISH

SUPERHERO QUALITY:
GREEDY MINI-MONSTER

SUPER STATS:
SCIENTIFIC NAME: *Megalodicopia hians*
Size: approx. 5 inches (13 centimeters)
Lifespan: 2 years
Habitat: deep sea
Location: Monterey Canyon, California

SUPER FACT:
The ghostfish has an adjustable mouth
rather like a mobile periscope.

**Ghostfish live up to 33,000 feet (10,000
meters) deep off the coast of northern
California, where there's no light!**

Anchored to rocks on the seabed, the ghostfish
opens its giant mouth, allowing water and tiny
prey to flow in. Then it quickly closes its mouth,
trapping any prey, and digests its prisoners. In the
same way that a carnivorous plant, such as a Venus
flytrap, snaps shut on insects, the ghostfish traps
a whole meal in one go, only opening its mouth
when it wants another meal.

While they fit within the invertebrate category of
"creatures without backbones," scientists have
noticed some similarities with vertebrates; the
larvae have a rod or "cord" instead of a backbone.
Could they actually be our own distant cousins?

STAR-NOSED MOLE

💪 SUPERHERO QUALITY:
SUPER-SNIFFER

💡 SUPER STATS:
SCIENTIFIC NAME: *Condylura cristata*
Size: 8 inches (20 centimeters)
Muzzle: 22 fleshy tentacles
Lifespan: 3 years
Location: eastern Canada and North America

✊ SUPER FACT:
The star-nosed mole can smell and find prey even underwater!

This North American mole has 22 strange, tentaclelike appendages attached to its snout. It uses some of them like fingers!

The mole's super-sensitive feelers are equipped with 25,000 sensory receptors that allow it to explore its environment. Like all moles, it is practically blind, so it finds prey—such as worms and aquatic insects—using its nose. It uses the longest of its appendages to locate its prey, and the shorter ones to carry the prey to its mouth. In the middle of the star shape is a super-sensitive zone that can detect even the tiniest vibrations.

The star-nosed mole is also famous for the speed with which it can catch prey, estimated to be a quarter of a second. No prey stands a chance of escaping the blind star-nosed mole!

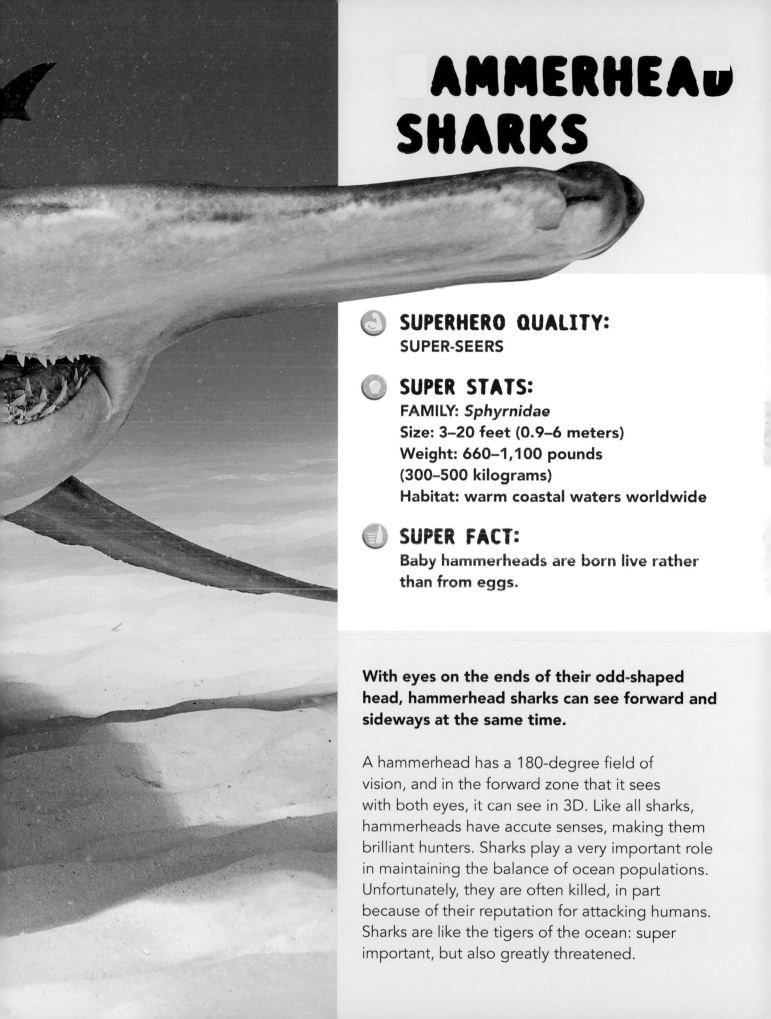

AMMERHEAD SHARKS

SUPERHERO QUALITY:
SUPER-SEERS

SUPER STATS:
FAMILY: *Sphyrnidae*
Size: 3–20 feet (0.9–6 meters)
Weight: 660–1,100 pounds
(300–500 kilograms)
Habitat: warm coastal waters worldwide

SUPER FACT:
Baby hammerheads are born live rather than from eggs.

With eyes on the ends of their odd-shaped head, hammerhead sharks can see forward and sideways at the same time.

A hammerhead has a 180-degree field of vision, and in the forward zone that it sees with both eyes, it can see in 3D. Like all sharks, hammerheads have accute senses, making them brilliant hunters. Sharks play a very important role in maintaining the balance of ocean populations. Unfortunately, they are often killed, in part because of their reputation for attacking humans. Sharks are like the tigers of the ocean: super important, but also greatly threatened.

NORTHERN GLASS FROG

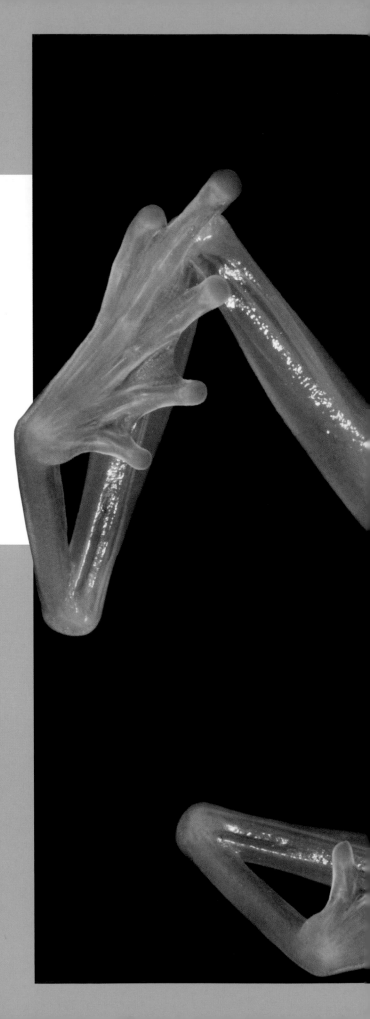

🐾 **SUPERHERO QUALITY:**
SEE-THROUGH SKIN

💡 **SUPER STATS:**
SCIENTIFIC NAME: *Hyalinobatrachium fleischmanni*
Size: 0.8–1.5 inches (2–3.8 centimeters)
Habitat: rainforest
Location: mostly Ecuador, Colombia, Venezuela and southern Central America

👍 **SUPER FACT:**
It's the male rather than the female that looks after the eggs.

You can see right through this glass frog!

Its belly is transparent! This means you can see everything inside it: skeleton, digestive tract, circulatory system, and lungs. You'd have to look closely, though, as it is less than 1.5 inches long!

Why is the glass frog see-through? Could it be a kind of camouflage, since it makes the frog almost invisible? Or is it an adaptation of the skin to protect it from the harsh rays of the sun? Scientists can't agree.

This species of glass frog lives in the Amazon rainforest, which is being destroyed at a rapid rate by farming, deforestation, and urbanization. Due to habitat loss, there has been a decline in numbers of this curious creature.

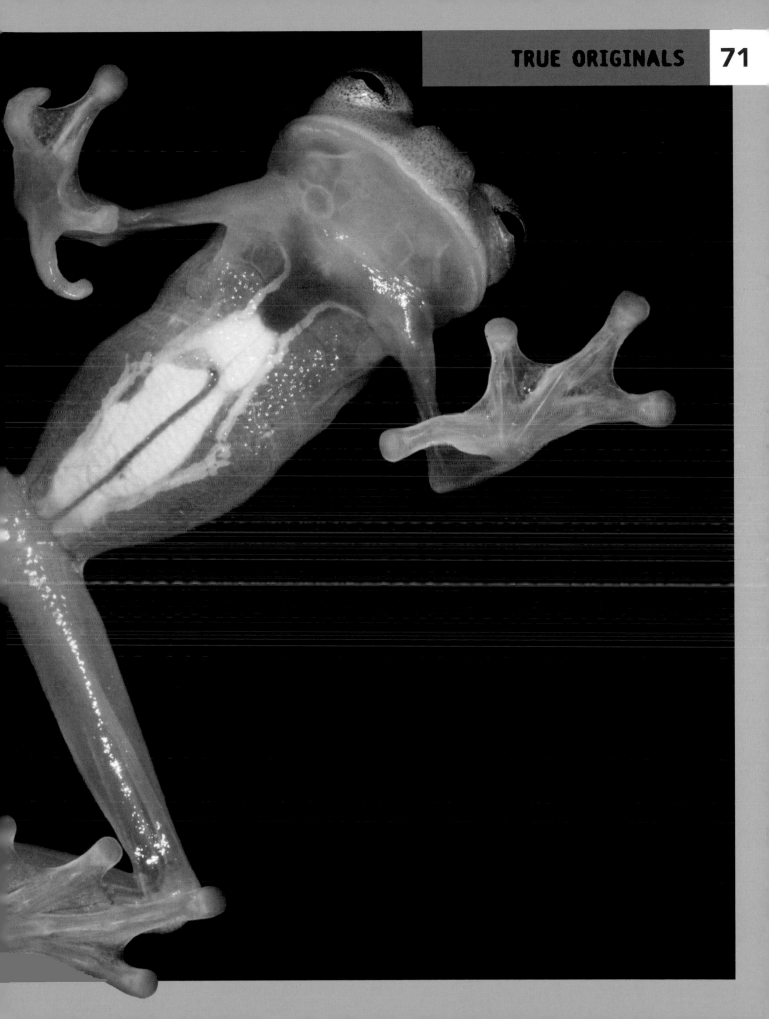

SEA CUCUMBERS

💪 **SUPERHERO QUALITY:**
TRANSFORMERS

💡 **SUPER STATS:**
PHYLUM: Echinodermata
Size: normally 4–12 inches (10–30 centimeters), but some species can be longer than 10 feet (3 meters)
Habitat: any depth of the sea

👍 **SUPER FACT:**
Some sea cucumbers send out white threads, called "Cuvier tubes," to engulf anything that comes too near.

Despite their name, sea cucumbers are animals, not vegetables. They belong to a group called "echinoderms," and are distant cousins of starfish and sea urchins.

The species shown, *Bohadschia graeffei*, has a ring of tentacles around its mouth used for feeding. If a predator approaches a little too close, the sea cucumber can move away by expelling water. Some species send out toxic sticky threads to trap their enemies. If this doesn't work, they can expel their digestive tube from inside their body so they can hide behind it while they slip away into cracks in the rocks. The organ takes several days to regrow. Sea cucumbers have one more defensive trick up their sleeve. Collagen fibers form a kind of shell around their body. By making these go rigid, they become hard as rock. Try eating that!

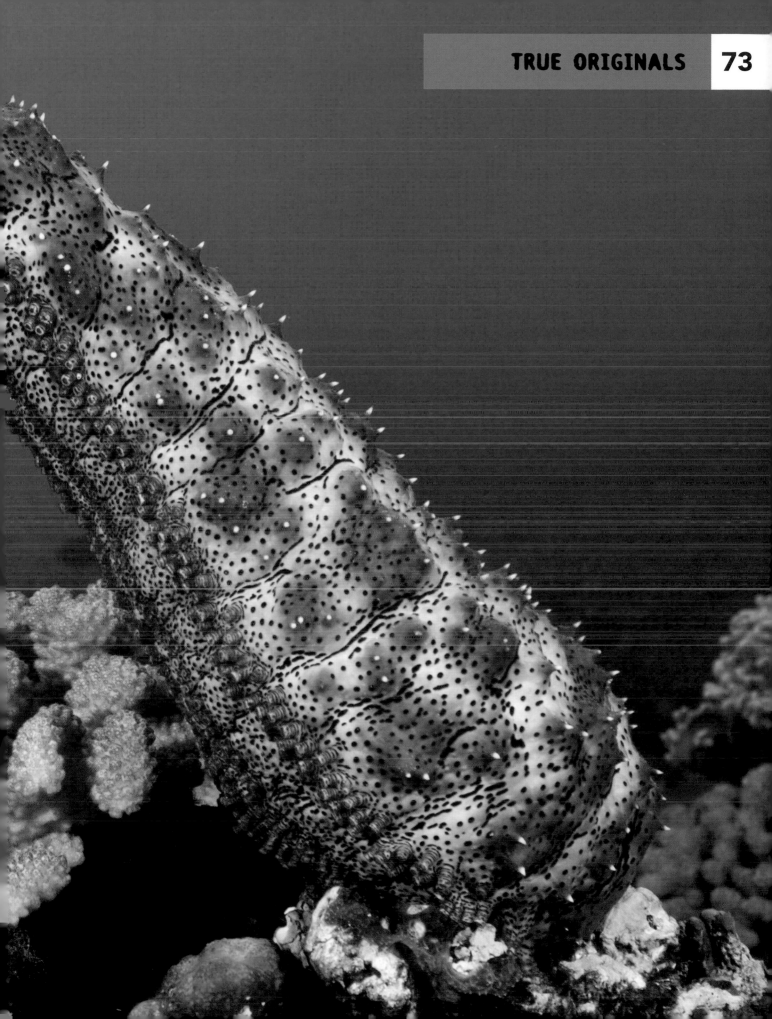

IMMORTAL JELLYFISH

 **SUPERHERO QUALITY:**
FOREVER YOUNG

 SUPER STATS:
SCIENTIFIC NAME:
Turritopsis dohrnii
Size: 0.4 inch (1 centimeter) diameter
Lifespan: infinite
Location: Japan and the Mediterranean Sea

SUPER FACT:
This is the only animal in the world that can reverse its life cycle.

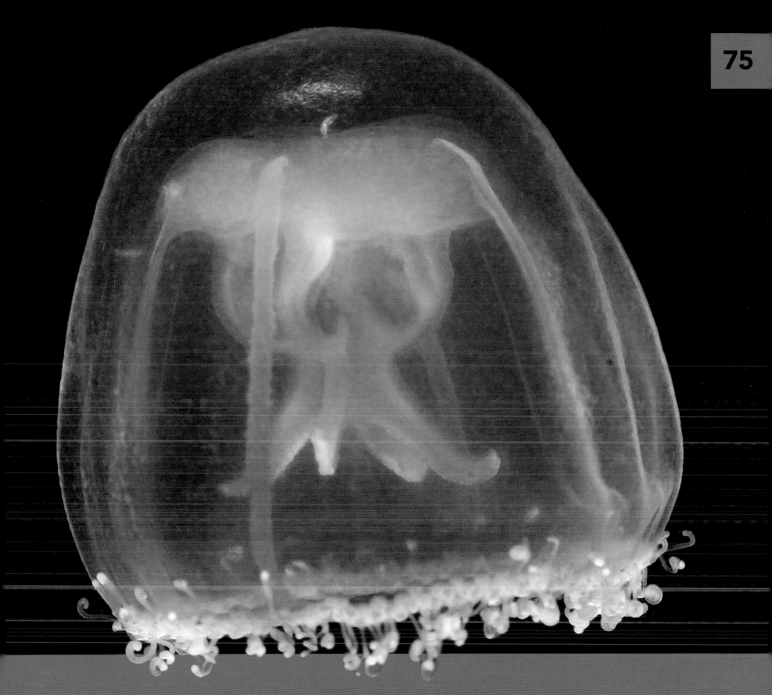

The immortal jellyfish may get eaten by a predator or washed up on a beach, but it will never die of old age!

How is this possible? To understand it, first you need to know something about a jellyfish's life cycle. All jellyfish start life as a "planula larva," a blob floating free in the ocean. As soon as the planula finds something it can attach to, like a rock, it fixes itself there and grows a stalk with tentacles at the top. In its new "polyp" phase, it looks like a tiny anemone stuck to a rock. As it grows, new polyps grow or "bud" from it. Eventually, the polyps detach from the rock and become tiny free-floating jellyfish (known as medusa).

What's special about the immortal jellyfish is that if it is attacked or starving or stressed by its environment, instead of dying it can decide to convert its cells backward, so it becomes a polyp again. It's rather as if an elderly hen turned back into an egg, or a butterfly became a caterpillar again!

REBELS

Which is most impressive, the flying snake or the flying frog, the walking fish or the wingless bird? These unusual stars of the animal world have played with evolution, rebelling against the norms of their species in some surprising ways. But they all share one aim: to keep on living on this planet wherever they still can.

FLYING DRAGONS

SUPERHERO QUALITY:
LIZARDS OF THE SKY

SUPER STATS:
FAMILY: *Agamidae*
Size inc. tail: 7–9 inches (19–23 centimeters)
Habitat: Asiatic rainforests
Location: south Asia, east Asia,
Southeast Asia

SUPER FACT:
The flying dragon is actually a lizard.

This creature is the grain of truth behind the mythical winged dragon that can fly!

To call it a "flying" dragon is a little misleading, though, as it doesn't actually have wings. Instead, it has wide membranes of skin attached to its ribs. When it extends its ribs, the skin unfurls and catches the air, allowing the dragon to glide for 33 feet (10 meters), and occasionally a lot more, between trees. The two winglike membranes are often vibrantly colored, unlike the rest of its body.

When the flying dragon is at rest, with its "wings" folded away, it's not very scary at all, except perhaps to its favorite food, ants and termites, which it catches with its sticky tongue. As for breathing fire, that's for fairy-tales! Sadly, though, flying dragons do not live in a fairy-tale world, and their natural habitat is being rapidly destroyed by humans.

WALLACE'S FLYING FROG

 **SUPERHERO QUALITY:**
AIRBORNE AMPHIBIAN

 **SUPER STATS:**
SCIENTIFIC NAME:
Rhacophorus nigropalmatus
FAMILY: *Rhacophoridae*
Size (adult): 2–4 inches
(5–11 centimeters)
Habitat: trees

 SUPER FACT:
This frog is named for the biologist Alfred Russel Wallace, whose theories of evolution were published with Charles Darwin's.

This little frog from Southeast Asia uses its enormous flippers to fly!

Its flippers are actually membranes stretched between its fingers. Because it has four of these flippers, it has four times the lift, enough to carry its superlight body from branch to branch. The distance it can glide is only a few feet, but that's usually enough for it to get away from predators or to approach prey, such as insects, snails, and even small birds.

During the mating season, the male woos the female with his song. Sometimes these tropical frogs actually mate in the air! Then, perched on a branch above a lake, the female produces a bubbly nest for her eggs or frogspawn. As the tadpoles start to hatch and move about, they burst the bubbles and fall with a whoosh straight into the water below; no wings or parachute for their first flight! Three weeks later, the little tadpoles have turned into fully-fledged flying frogs with flippers of their own.

RE -LI E SH
ROSY-LIPPED
BATFISH

SUPERHERO QUALITY:
WALKING FISH

SUPER STATS:
SCIENTIFIC NAMES: *Ogcocephalus darwini* (red-lipped) / *Ogcocephalus porrectus* (rosy-lipped)
Size: 6–8 inches (15–20 centimeters)
Habitat: seabed
Location: Galapagos and Costa Rica

SUPER FACT:
These walking fish know how to hide in plain sight.

These bizarre red- and rosy-lipped fish would rather walk than swim!

They move across the seabed on their pectoral fins, which they use like legs. The red-lipped batfish lives near the Galapagos islands, while the rosy-lipped batfish lives off Costa Rica. They are named "batfish" because their large, outstretched fins look rather like wings.

By pivoting on its fins, the batfish is able to move slowly toward its prey. When it gets near, it stays completely still, huddled against a rock or partly hidden in the sand, and dangles a "lure" above its mouth that emits a bright light. The lure looks like bait, and attracts little fish, crustaceans, and sea worms close enough for the batfish to catch.

NAMIB SAND GECKO

SUPERHERO QUALITY:
SURFER OF THE SANDS

SUPER STATS:
SCIENTIFIC NAME:
Palmatogecko rangei
FAMILY: *Gekkonidae*
Size: 5–5.5 inches
(12–14 centimeters)
Habitat: desert
Location: southeast Africa

SUPER FACT:
The Namib sand gecko can move very fast across sand, using its feet like mini-surfboards!

This little lizard lives in the Namib desert, where it "surfs" across the sand at night on webbed feet!

The desert in Namibia can get very hot in the daytime. Most of the creatures that live there—including the Namib sand gecko—spend the day sheltering from the sun. Using its webbed feet, it digs a burrow where it can keep cool and enjoy the moisture that condenses on the walls. At night, this strictly nocturnal creature emerges from its burrow and climbs the dunes in search of prey. Its webbed feet prevent it from sinking into the sand, and little adhesive pads on its toes help it climb. The gecko feeds on crickets, grasshoppers, and small spiders, which are all it needs to stay alive.

In the morning, the Namib sand gecko collects any drops of dew that have gathered on its huge, oversized, red-and-brown eyeballs using… its own tongue! Lacking eyelids, it needs to lick its eyes occasionally to clean them.

VERREAUX'S SIFAKA

🦾 **SUPERHERO QUALITY:**
TWO-LEGGED SHUFFLER

💡 **SUPER STATS:**
SCIENTIFIC NAME: *Propithecus verreauxi*
FAMILY: *Indridae*
Size: 18 inches (45 centimeters) not inc. tail
Weight: 77 pounds (3.5 kilograms)
Habitat: Asiatic rainforests
Location: southwest Madagascar

👍 **SUPER FACT:**
This adorable species lives in groups of 4–8.

Verreaux's sifaka prefers to be in the trees, but when it does come down to the ground it moves in a very unusual way! Its feet bound from side to side, like a goalkeeper moving along the line!

It does this special move in every kind of forest environment in Madagascar, where it is now highly endangered.

This beautiful creature, a member of the lemur family, has a thick, white fur coat with brown patches, and a very long tail, which it uses as a balance. It rests during the hottest part of the day and spends the mornings and evenings jumping skilfully between the branches looking for food. Using its strong back legs, it pushes off from the tree trunks and propels itself through the air a distance of up to 30 feet (9 meters)!

PHILIPPINE FLYING LEMUR

💪 **SUPERHERO QUALITY:**
SKY-DWELLING MAMMAL

💡 **SUPER STATS:**
SCIENTIFIC NAME: *Cynocephalus volans*
Size: 30–37 inches (77–95 centimeters)
Weight: 2.2–4 pounds (1–1.8 kilograms)
Lifespan: 15–20 years
Habitat: tropical rainforests of Southeast Asia

👍 **SUPER FACT:**
These mammals can glide up to
500 feet (150 meters)!

The extraordinary Philippine flying lemur never touches the ground!

Instead, it uses a membrane of skin to "parachute" between trees. Called a patagium, the membrane extends from its chin to the end of its tail, passing through its fingers and toes and giving it incredible flying abilities.

Scientists have struggled to agree on how to classify this animal. It was first categorized as being in the order Chiroptera, which includes bats, but it was later compared more to flying squirrels, and then later still to lemurs, which have the same pointed snout and tree-dwelling habits. Now, genetic research has put them in a different order, Dermoptera, whose closest relatives are primates. They're like our cousins!

PARADISE FLYING SNAKE

 SUPERHERO QUALITY:
TREETOP REPTILE

 **SUPER STATS:**
SCIENTIFIC NAME:
Chrysopelea paradisi
FAMILY: *Colubridae*
Size: 3–5 feet (1–1.5 meters)
Habitat: tropical rainforests of Southeast Asia

 SUPER FACT:
This snake throws itself into the air like a throwing disk!

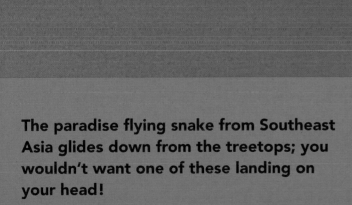

The paradise flying snake from Southeast Asia glides down from the treetops; you wouldn't want one of these landing on your head!

Fixing its body in one position, it "flies" from branch to branch to capture prey. To do this, it splays its ribs, giving its body a greater surface area and thus more air resistance. Inching slowly to the very edge of a branch, it curves its body into an S-shape, the ideal shape for flying.

Using these techniques, it can travel about 330 feet (100 meters) through the air before it lands on another branch; that's a long way!

As with many species in the rainforests of Southeast Asia, the paradise flying snake is threatened by deforestation, which is regrettably continuing at a rapid pace.

AFRICAN WILD DOG

SUPERHERO QUALITY:
BOTH WOLF AND HYENA!

SUPER STATS:
SCIENTIFIC NAME: *Lycaon pictus*
FAMILY: *Canidae*
Size: 27–31 inches (70–80 centimeters)
Weight: 44–66 pounds (20–30 kilograms)
Location: Southern and central
sub-Saharan Africa

SUPER FACT:
A pack can run long distances at 15 miles per hour (25 kilometers per hour) to find prey!

The African wild dog has the habits of a wolf, but with its arched back, short neck, and powerful jaws, it looks more like a hyena.

Like wolves, these dogs live in packs of 5 to 20 individuals. Each pack has a dominant pair and a clear social structure. The older members closely guard the young, and the young show them respect. Each dog has its own smell and its own unique voice; it gives little cries and moans that mark it out within the family. It also has its own unique, blotchy markings, hence the nickname "painted wolf."

Like wolves, these dogs hunt for prey rather than scavenging. The pack approaches silently; then, with a signal from the dominant male, it gives chase. When the prey tires of running, the dogs attack.

REEF MANTA RAY

 **SUPERHERO QUALITY:**
GLIDING FISH

 SUPER STATS:
SCIENTIFIC NAME: *Mobula alfredi*
FAMILY: *Mobulidae*
Size: 10–16 feet (3–5 meters) across
Habitat: tropical and subtropical coastal waters

SUPER FACT:
Manta rays can leap out of the water as well as gliding underwater.

The reef manta ray must keep swimming at all times in order to breathe; this keeps its blood circulating in its gills.

Any diver lucky enough to spot this manta ray in tropical waters will be stunned by its gracefulness. With its huge pectoral fins, it appears to fly through the water! It feeds mostly on zooplankton and little crustaceans, which it ingests by opening its mouth wide when it's on the move. When feeding, it channels water into its mouth using a pair of fins on either side of its mouth. When swimming, it rolls these fins into a tube shape.

The reef manta ray is one of the largest ray species. Largest of all is the giant oceanic manta ray. Both species are closely related to the nine species of mobula ray. Mantas behave differently depending on where they live. In deep water, they move in a straight line at a steady speed. Nearer the coast, they move in more of a wave motion, slowing down and speeding up again as they swim.

FLIGHTLESS CORMORANT

SUPERHERO QUALITY:
THIS BIRD HAS NO WINGS

SUPER STATS:
SCIENTIFIC NAME: *Phalacrocorax harrisi*
Size: 35–39 inches (90–100 centimeters)
Weight: 5.5–11 pounds (2.5–5 kilograms)
Location: Galapagos archipelago

SUPER FACT:
The flightless cormorant's feathers are denser and softer than those of other birds, and look more like hair.

Charles Darwin met these flightless birds, which are stuck on land!

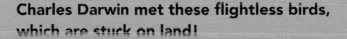

If you want to see one, you'd have to go to the Galapagos islands off the coast of Ecuador. The discovery of these flightless birds reinforced Darwin's theory of evolution. The likely story, he thought, was that cormorants from South America flew to the Galapagos and landed there. With the passing of time, because they lived so peacefully on the island and were safe from any predators, they lost their ability to fly. If a bird can survive on land without competition or threat, why look to the skies for an escape route?

The flightless cormorant's wings are too small to be used as flippers. Instead, this bird moves through the water using its webbed feet. It may not be able to fly, but it's very good at diving!

Brimming with creative inspiration, how-to projects, and useful information to enrich your everyday life, quarto.com is a favorite destination for those pursuing their interests and passions.

Inspiring | Educating | Creating | Entertaining

Text © 2022 Quarto Publishing Group USA Inc.
Adapted from original French language text
© 2022 Belles Balades Editions

First published in 2022 by QEB Publishing,
an imprint of The Quarto Group.
100 Cummings Center,
Suite 265D Beverly,
MA 01915, USA.
T (978) 282-9590 F (978) 283-2742
www.quarto.com

Editorial Assistant: Alice Hobbs
Editor: Amber Husain
Design: Starry Dog
Art Director: Susi Martin
Publisher: Holly Willsher

A CIP record for this book is available from the Library of Congress.

ISBN: 978-0-7112-8000-7

9 8 7 6 5 4 3 2 1

Manufactured in Guangdong, China TT062022

MIX
Paper from responsible sources
FSC® C016973

PICTURE CREDITS

Adobe Stock Photo: 22/23 hakoar; 32/33 gudkovandrey; 68/69 wild-estanimal. **Alamy:** 16/17 Afripics / Alamy Stock Photo; 26/27 Redmond Durrell / Alamy Stock Photo; 48/49 Rick & Nora Bowers; 86/87 Joshua Davenport. **Biosphoto:** Front cover: Martin Harvey; 10/11 © Luciano Candisani / Minden Pictures; 14/15 © Fred Bavendam / Minden Pictures; 24/25 © Paulo de Oliveira / Biosphoto; 34/35 © Martin Harvey; 44/45 © Adam Fletcher; 52/53 © Michael Durham / Minden Pictures; 56/57 © Reinhard Dirscherl; 60/61 © Sylvain Cordier; 62/63 © Husni Che Ngah; 64/65 © Norbert Wu / Minden Pictures; 66/67 © Ken Catania / Visuals Unlimited / SPL - Science Photo Library / Biosphoto; 70/71 © Pete Oxford / Minden Pictures; 72/73 © Reinhard Dirscherl; 74/75 © Ryo Minemizu / Oasis; 76/77 © Chien Lee / Minden Pictures; 78/79 © Quentin Martinez; 80/81 © Fred Bavendam / Minden Pictures / Biosphoto; 82/83 © Martin Harvey; 88/89 © Cede Prudente / Photoshot /Biosphoto; 92/93 © Tim Fitzharris / Minden Pictures. **Hemis.fr:** 18/19 © Minden / Alamy / Hemis; 20/21 © Minden / Alamy / Hemis; 40/41 © Robert Harding / hemis.fr; 94/95 © Minden. **Nature Picture Library:** 6/7 Rolf Nussbaumer; 12/13 Nature Production; 30/31 Francois Savigny; 36/37 Juan Manuel Borrero; 38/39 Jeff Foott; 58/59 Sergey Gorshkov; 84/85 Andy Rouse; 90/91 Wim van den Heever. **Shutterstock:** Back cover (top) Wang LiQiang; (center b/g) Tunatura; (center f/g) Rich Carey; (bottom left) Ryan M. Bolton; (bottom right) Hariyono Suwardi; 1 Hariyono Suwardi; 2/3 Dotted Yeti; 4/5 Ethan Daniels; 8/9 YIUCHEUNG; 28/29 Jackal photography; 42/43 © Jiri Prochazka; 46/47 Michiel Scheerhoorn; 50/51 Hein Myers Photography; 54/55 Marek R. Swadzba; 96 Denis Moskvinov.